DATE DUE

Capstone Short Biographies

African-American Aviators

Bessie Coleman, William J. Powell,
James Herman Banning, Benjamin O. Davis Jr.,
General Daniel James Jr.

by Dr. Stanley P. Jones

Content Advisor:
Kenneth O. Wofford
WWII pilot graduate, Tuskegee Army Air Field
U. S. Air Force (ret.)

CAPSTONE
HIGH/LOW BOOKS
an imprint of Capstone Press

C A P S T O N E   P R E S S

818 North Willow Street • Mankato, MN 56001

http://www.capstone-press.com

Library of Congress Cataloging-in-Publication Data
Jones, Stanley P., 1956-
   African-American aviators: James Herman Banning, Bessie Coleman, General Daniel "Chappie" James Jr., Benjamin O. Davis Jr., William J. Powell/by Stanley P. Jones.
   p. cm. (Capstone short biographies)
   Includes bibliographical references and index.
   Summary: Briefly describes the lives and accomplishments of five African American pilots: James Banning, Bessie Coleman, Daniel James, Benjamin Davis, and William Powell.
   ISBN 1-56065-696-4
   1. Afro-American air pilots--Juvenile literature. [1. Afro-American air pilots. 2. Air pilots. 3. Afro-Americans-Biography.] I. Title. II. Series.
TL539.J66 1998
629.13'092'273
[B]--DC21

97-40176
CIP
AC

Editorial credits:
Editor, Rebecca Glaser; cover design, James Franklin; photo research, Michelle L. Norstad

Photo credits:
Archive Photos, 7, 8
Los Angeles Public Library, 24, 27, 28, 31
Museum of Flight Archives/Hatfield Collection, 18, 21, 23
Schomburg Center /New York Public Library, 4, 13, 43
Smithsonian Institution/National Air and Space Museum, 14, 16, 34, 38, 40
UPI/Corbis-Bettman, cover, 10, 37
U.S. Air Force, 32

Table of Contents

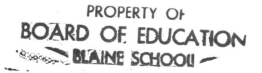

Chapter 1

What is an Aviator?

Aviators are operators or pilots of airplanes. Aviators must study, train, practice, and take tests before they receive their pilots' licenses. A pilot's license is a paper giving a person official permission to fly a plane.

Training

Student pilots take flight training classes to learn how airplane systems operate. These classes are called ground school. Student pilots learn how weather affects plane flight and how to use maps. They learn how to use two-way radios to communicate with airports. Communicate means to share facts and knowledge.

Student pilots fly with flight instructors during flight training. They learn how to take

Aviators are operators or pilots of airplanes.

off, fly, and land. They fly alone when they have completed enough training.

The Federal Aviation Administration (FAA) makes rules about flying. The rules make flying safer for pilots. The FAA gives written tests to student pilots after they complete training. Student pilots also take an oral test and a flight test. They receive their licenses when they pass all the tests.

Aviation History

The Wright Brothers built and flew the first working airplane in 1903. Flying was risky. Early pilots did not always use parachutes or seat belts. A parachute is a large piece of strong, light cloth. It lets a person float slowly and safely to the ground. People tried to improve airplanes to make them safer. They built new planes that were lighter, stronger, and faster.

Governments began using planes in the military during World War I (1914-1918). The U.S. government started the U.S. Army Air Corps. The Army Air Force became a separate major branch of the military in 1947.

The Wright Brothers built the first working airplane in 1903.

Los Angeles became a center for aviation during World War I. Manufacturers produced many planes there. After the war, the Army had more airplanes than it needed. The Army sold some planes to civilians. A civilian is a person who is not in the military.

More people became interested in flying because more planes were available. Pilots appeared at county fairs and circuses. They

Many stunt pilots flew the Curtiss 4N-J.

performed stunts in air shows. A stunt is an act that shows great skill or daring. Stunts usually involve danger. Many stunt pilots flew the Curtiss 4N-J. Pilots called it a Jenny for short.

Aviation became more popular. Many flying clubs and schools formed during the 1920s and 1930s. Some pilots carried mail on planes. Others carried passengers.

African-American Pilots

Many African Americans wanted to fly airplanes, too. But most U.S. flight schools would not admit African Americans in the 1920s and 1930s. Some traveled to France to obtain pilot's licenses. A few started aviation schools for African Americans in the United States.

The U.S military was segregated. Segregated means separated by race. African Americans could not command or supervise white soldiers.

African Americans could not serve as military pilots until 1941. The Army started the first African-American unit of the air corps in Tuskegee, Alabama. A unit is a small group within a larger group.

The pilots from Tuskegee did not serve in combat until 1943. Later, the members of this unit were called the Tuskegee Airmen of World War II (1939-1945). They performed well in combat.

Segregation in the military officially ended in 1948. President Harry Truman ordered the military to treat all people equally.

Chapter 2

Bessie Coleman

1893-1926

Bessie Coleman was born January 26, 1893, in Atlanta, Texas. She had five older brothers and three younger sisters. Her parents were sharecroppers. Sharecroppers are farmers who do not own land. They work on someone's land in exchange for food, shelter, and part of the crop.

Coleman's father moved to Oklahoma when she was seven years old. She stayed in Texas with her mother.

Coleman picked cotton with her family. She took care of her younger sisters. She did not attend school regularly. But she loved books and read everything she could.

Bessie Coleman was the first licensed African-American pilot in the United States.

Learning and Working

Coleman attended the Colored Agricultural and Normal University in Langston, Oklahoma. She was placed in a preparatory program because she did not meet all the requirements. Coleman did not have enough money to stay in school. She had to drop out after less than one year. She moved to Chicago where two of her older brothers lived.

Coleman trained to be a manicurist at a beauty school in Chicago. A manicurist is a person who trims and polishes fingernails. Coleman worked in barber shops. She fixed men's nails. She met many people and heard stories about flying. She wanted to learn how to fly.

The Quest to Fly

Newspaper stories about Eugene Bullard inspired Coleman. Eugene Bullard was an African American. Bullard moved to France. He served as a pilot in the French army during World War I.

Coleman could not learn to fly in the United States because she was an African American.

Coleman could not learn to fly in the United States because she was an African American. No U.S. flight schools would admit African Americans. Few people thought women of any race should fly. Most people thought flying was too risky for women.

Coleman met Robert Abbott while working at the barbershop. Abbott owned a newspaper.

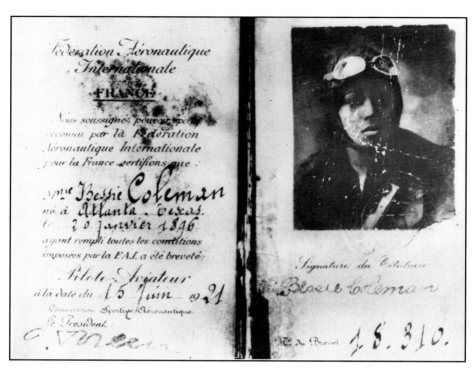

**Coleman received her pilot's license from the
Federation Aeronautique Internationale in 1921.**

He thought that stories about an African-
American woman pilot would sell copies of his
paper. Abbott helped Coleman find a flying
school in France.

Coleman became manager of a chili
restaurant so she could earn money to go to
France. A restaurant is a place that serves food.
Coleman also took French lessons.

Flying in France

Coleman went to France in November of 1920. She took flying lessons at the Ecole d'Aviation des Freres Caudron. In French, this name means the Aviation School of the Caudron Brothers. It was France's most famous flight school.

Coleman lived in France for ten months. She took her pilot's license test after completing her training. The Federation Aeronautique Internationale (International Federation of Aviation) granted her a license on June 15, 1921. Coleman became the first African American to earn a pilot's license.

Back in the United States

Coleman sailed back to the United States. Robert Abbott printed stories about her in the Chicago *Defender* newspaper. Many reporters came to New York to interview her when she got off the ship. Coleman dreamed of opening a flight school for African Americans. She wanted African Americans to have a place where they could learn to fly.

Coleman started performing in air shows. She began to barnstorm. Barnstorm means to tour the country performing airplane stunts. Barnstormers performed stunts like wing-walking, parachute jumping, and flying in loops.

Barnstormers often appeared at county fairs. They took many risks. They often used old planes that were not safe. Some barnstormers died when their planes crashed.

Coleman died on April 30, 1926, when her plane crashed. She was practicing for an air show in Jacksonville, Florida. She was not wearing a parachute or a seat belt. Coleman achieved her dream of becoming a pilot. She became a role model for future African-American aviators.

Bessie Coleman achieved her dream of becoming a pilot.

Chapter 3

William J. Powell

1899-1942

William J. Powell was born in Henderson, Kentucky, in July 1899. His family moved to Chicago when he was eight years old. He graduated from Wendell Phillips High School at age 16.

Powell attended the University of Illinois after high school. He studied engineering. Engineering is the science of planning and building machines, automobiles, and structures.

In 1917, Powell began army officer training school in Chilicothe, Ohio. At that time, the military was segregated. Powell's unit was made up of only African Americans. He received the rank of first lieutenant. He fought

William J. Powell wanted African Americans to be involved in all areas of aviation.

in Europe in World War I (1914-1918). The enemy attacked Powell's unit with poison gas. He became very sick. He returned to the United States to get well.

Powell never completely recovered from the poison gas. But he was well enough to open a service station in Chicago. Powell's business was so successful that he built three more service stations.

The Birth of a Dream

Powell traveled to Paris, France, in 1927. He took his first airplane ride there. The flight changed his life. He wanted to become a pilot.

Powell knew aviation would be important in the future. He realized that planes could be used for moving goods and people. He hoped African Americans could become involved in all areas of aviation.

Powell tried to enter a flying school when he returned to Chicago. But no flying school in Chicago would accept African Americans. Powell did not give up. He wrote to other

The Bessie Coleman Aero Club owned a workshop where members could build and repair planes.

schools in the United States. Finally, a flying school in Los Angeles accepted him. It was the the Warren College of Aeronautics. He sold his garage and service stations. He moved to Los Angeles in 1928.

Powell studied hard for his pilot's license. He learned the flying rules set up by the U.S. Department of Commerce. He practiced flying for many hours. Powell received his pilot's license in 1928.

Bessie Coleman Aero Club

Powell started an aviation club for African Americans. He asked businessmen, mechanics, and other pilots to join the club. They formed the Bessie Coleman Aero Club in 1929. It was the first African-American aviation club. The club provided pilot training. It owned a workshop where members could build and repair planes.

The Bessie Coleman Aero Club had trouble raising enough money at first. But the club became successful. It sponsored the first African-American air show on Labor Day in 1931. There were five African-American pilots in the air show. They called themselves the Five Blackbirds. The show was so successful that they had a second show in December. The Bessie Coleman Aero Club helped more African Americans to become pilots.

Powell also belonged to an organization called the Craftsmen of Black Wings, Inc. They published a newsletter called *Craftsmen-Aero*

The Bessie Coleman Aero Club sponsored African-American air shows.

News. Powell wrote many articles about his vision for African Americans in aviation. Powell also wrote a book called *Black Wings* to get African Americans interested in aviation.

Powell died in 1942 at a veterans' hospital in Sharon, Wyoming. No one knows much about his sickness and death. His sickness was probably related to his World War I injuries, however.

Chapter 4

James Herman Banning

1900-1933

James Herman Banning was born in Canton, Oklahoma on November 5, 1900. Banning was the youngest of four children. His parents were farmers.

As a child, Banning enjoyed math and reading. He liked to look at pictures in books. He liked to work with machines on his parents' farm. Banning watched films about World War I (1914-1918). He enjoyed watching the fighter planes. He wanted to learn more about airplanes.

Learning and Working

Banning left Oklahoma in 1919. He went to Iowa State College in Ames, Iowa. Banning's parents moved to Iowa to be with him.

James Herman Banning became the chief flight instructor at the Bessie Coleman Aero Club.

Banning opened an automobile repair shop in Ames while he was in college. He continued to read and learn everything he could about airplanes. In 1920, he rode in an airplane for the first time. He paid $5 for the ride at a circus. After the ride, Banning started dreaming of becoming a pilot.

Banning's auto repair shop did well. He left college so he could operate his business full-time. But he still wanted to fly.

Banning could not find a flying school where he could take lessons. No flight school in the United States would accept African Americans. Finally, Banning met a former World War I pilot named Lieutenant Raymond C. Fisher. Fisher taught him how to fly.

Buying an Airplane

In 1926, the U.S. Department of Commerce established air licensing laws. Banning was the first African American licensed by the U.S. Department of Commerce.

Banning bought his own airplane. It was a Hummingbird biplane. A biplane is an airplane

A biplane is an airplane with two sets of wings.

with two sets of wings. He named his plane
Miss Ames. He flew Miss Ames all around the
country. Banning became a barnstormer like
Bessie Coleman. He performed at air shows.
He also carried mail.

African Americans wanted a member of
their race to make a cross-country flight. Many
white people did not think African Americans
were capable pilots. Flying across the country

would prove that African Americans were serious about aviation. African Americans had only made shorter flights so far.

Cross-Country Flight

Banning moved to Los Angeles. He met aviator William J. Powell. Powell asked him to join the Bessie Coleman Aero Club. Banning became the club's chief instructor. He was the most experienced pilot in the club.

Banning wanted to buy a new airplane. But he could not afford one. Instead, he bought a used biplane with a 14-year-old engine. The plane was an Eagle Rock from World War I. He met a mechanic named Thomas C. Allen who helped him fix the airplane.

Banning and Allen wanted to make a cross-country flight. They decided to try it in the Eagle Rock. They planned to make several stops during the trip.

Banning and Allen decided to ask African Americans for money along the way. They needed money for oil, gas, food, and lodging.

Banning named his first airplane Miss Ames.

They had only about $100 at the start of their trip. This was not enough money to fly from California to New York. Banning and Allen called themselves the Flying Hobos. A hobo is someone who travels from place to place with little money.

They left Los Angeles, California, on September 18, 1932. They looked for African Americans wherever they landed. African Americans gave them food and money. They stopped and visited relatives along the way.

Banning and Allen made many stops. The trip took them three weeks. But they were in the air less than 42 hours. On October 9, 1932, the Eagle Rock landed in Valley Stream, Long Island. They had flown from California to the east coast.

Banning and Allen became the first African Americans to fly across the country. They proved that African Americans were capable of long flights. They received awards from New York City and the city of Los Angeles.

FIRST TRANS-CONTINENTAL FLIGHT
Los Angeles to New York
October 9th 1932   Flying time 41 hrs 27 min.

J. Herman Banning
Pilot

Thomas C. Allen,
Mec.

Banning and Allen were the first African Americans to fly across the country.

Banning died on February 5, 1933. He was a passenger in an airplane that crashed at an air show in San Diego, California. He lived just four months after completing his cross-country flight.

Chapter 5

Benjamin O. Davis Jr.

1912-

Benjamin O. Davis Jr. was born December 18, 1912, in Washington, D.C. His father was the first African-American general in the U.S. Army. His mother died when he was five years old. Davis lived with his grandparents in Washington, D.C., after his mother died.

The army assigned his father to a teaching job at Tuskegee Institute. Tuskegee Institute was a college for African Americans. Davis moved to Tuskegee, Alabama, to live with his father and stepmother. They later moved to Cleveland, Ohio.

In 1926, Davis and his father visited his relatives in Washington, D.C. He watched

Benjamin O. Davis Jr. was the first African American to become a lieutenant general in the Air Force.

Davis wanted to become a pilot.

acrobatic airplanes flying at a military air field.
An acrobatic airplane is a plane that can
perform stunts. His father paid $5 for Davis'
first airplane ride there.

    Davis began reading about Charles
Lindbergh's flight across the Atlantic Ocean.
Lindbergh was the first American to fly alone

across the Atlantic Ocean. Davis decided that he wanted to be a pilot.

Learning at West Point

Davis graduated at the top of his high school class. He began studying math at Case Western Reserve University in Cleveland. He wanted to learn to fly. But he could not find a flight school that would train African Americans.

Davis left Case Western Reserve University. He tried to get into the United States Military Academy at West Point, New York. He did not pass the entrance test. He studied for two months. He took the test again and passed.

Few African Americans attended West Point. Davis was lonely. The other students would not talk to him except in the line of duty. But Davis did not give up.

Davis graduated from West Point in June 1936. He was the first African American to graduate from West Point in the twentieth century. He wanted to become a pilot. He was qualified to enter the Army's training program. But the Army did not have any units for African-American pilots.

A Tuskegee Airman

Davis first served as an officer in a segregated army unit in Georgia. At that time, the military was segregated. In 1941, the Army created African-American units of the air corps. The army assigned these units to the air field in Tuskegee, Alabama.

Davis was in the first military pilot training class for African Americans. The class members graduated as fighter pilots. Many more African Americans became interested in pilot training. The army added more African-American flying units. It created the 332nd Fighter Group and the 477th Bomb Group. These groups were later known as the Tuskegee Airmen of World War II.

Davis became commander of the 99th Fighter Squadron and the supporting units. These units fought in North Africa, Italy, and the area around the Mediterranean Sea.

Davis later commanded the 332nd Fighter Group. The 332nd Group and the 99th Fighter Squadron fought together in Italy. All the airplanes in the 332nd had red tails.

The red tail fighter pilots flew escort missions to protect bombers from enemy fire.

Davis (right) commanded the 99th Fighter Squadron.

Bombers are planes that drop bombs. The pilots in the 332nd Fighter Group never lost a bomber they were escorting.

Davis had a successful military career after World War II. He held important positions in the U.S. Air Force. Davis was the first African American officer to be promoted to lieutenant general. He wore three stars on his uniform. He retired in 1970.

Chapter 6

General Daniel James Jr.

1920—1978

Daniel James Jr. was born February 11, 1920, in Pensacola, Florida. He was the youngest of 17 children. His nickname was Chappie. His older brother's nickname was also Chappie. James liked it and told people to call him Chappie, too.

James' father worked in a gas plant. His mother started a school for African Americans in their home. She taught James until he was in seventh grade.

James watched planes flying at the Pensacola Naval Air Station. He wanted to become a pilot. He did odd jobs at the airport. Pilots sometimes took James flying in

Daniel James Jr. was the first African American to become a four-star general.

James graduated from the Army Air Corps Cadet Program at the top of his class.

exchange for his work. James dreamed of flying for the navy. But the navy did not allow African Americans to become pilots at that time.

Learning and Working

James graduated from Washington High School in Pensacola. He attended college at Tuskegee Institute in Alabama. He met Dorothy Watkins there. They married in 1943.

James learned to fly during college. The Civilian Pilot Training Program trained people to fly. James became a flight instructor in this program.

James applied to the Army Air Corps Aviation Cadet Program. The military started the program in 1941 to train the first African-American military pilots. All of the military services were segregated at that time. James could not get into the Army Air Corps right away. The Army Air Corps would accept only a few African-American cadets.

In 1943, James became a cadet in the Army Air Corps. A cadet is a person who is training to be in the military. He later graduated from the Army Air Corps Cadet Program at the top of his class. James became a second lieutenant.

A Military Career

James learned to fly bombers. He also trained as a fighter pilot. He flew many missions. James was given a medal for bravery because he saved a pilot's life.

James served in many places during his military career. James received high military honors in the Air Force. He was a fighter pilot in the Korean War (1950-1953). He also flew in the Vietnam War (1954-1975). James gave many speeches while in the military. His speeches encouraged and inspired troops.

The military promoted James many times. On September 1, 1975, the Air Force made him a four-star general. This is the highest rank except for the general of the air force. Full generals wear four stars on their uniforms.

James retired from the United States Air Force on February 1, 1978. He had served his country for nearly 35 years. On February 25, 1978, he died from a heart attack.

James flew in the Korean and Vietnam Wars.

Words to Know

acrobatic airplane (ak-ruh-BAT-ik AIR-plane)—an airplane that can perform stunts

barnstorm (BARN-storm)—to tour the country performing airplane stunts

biplane (BYE-plane)—an airplane with two sets of wings, one above the other

bomber (BOM-ur)—a plane that drops bombs

manicurist (MAN-uh-kyur-ist)—a person who trims and polishes fingernails

pilot's license (PYE-luhts LYE-suhnss)—a paper giving a person official permission to fly a plane

segregated (SEG-ruh-gay-ted)—separated by race

sharecropper (SHAIR-krop-ur)—a person who works a piece of land for food, shelter, and part of the crop

stunt (stuhnt)—an act that shows great skill or daring

To Learn More

Hart, Philip S. *Flying Free: America's First Black Aviators*. Minneapolis: Lerner, 1992.

Hart, Philip S. *Up in the Air: The Story of Bessie Coleman*. Minneapolis: Carolrhoda Books, 1996.

Haskins, Jim. *Black Eagles: African Americans in Aviation*. New York: Scholastic, Inc., 1995.

McKissack, Patricia and Fredrick. *Red-tail Angels: The Story of the Tuskegee Airmen of World War II*. New York: Walker and Co., 1995.

Useful Addresses

International Civil Aviation Organization
External Relations and Public
   Information Office
999 University Street
Montreal, Quebec H3C 5H7
Canada

Organization of Black Airline Pilots
OBAP National Office
P.O. Box 50666
Phoenix, AZ 85076-0666

Tuskegee Airmen, Inc.
1 Massachusetts Avenue NW
Box 15
Washington, DC 20001

Internet Sites

Afro-American: The Tuskegee Airmen
http://www.afroam.org/history/tusk/
  tuskmain.html

Air Force Kids Online
http://www.af.mil/aflinkjr/entrance.htm

Organization of Black Airline Pilots
http://www.obap.org/

African-American History at the National Air and Space Museum
http://www.nasm.edu/NASMDOCS/PA/
  NASMNEWS/BHISTORY.HTM

Index

332nd Fighter Group, 36, 37
99th Fighter Squadron, 36

Abbott, Robert, 13, 14, 15
acrobatic airplane, 34
Allen, Thomas C., 29, 30
Army Air Corps, 6, 36, 41

barnstorm, 17, 27
Bessie Coleman Aero Club, 22-23, 29
biplane, 26, 29
bomber, 36, 37, 42
Bullard, Eugene, 12

cadet, 41
Chicago *Defender*, 15
Civilian Pilot Training Program, 41
Commerce, Department of, 21, 26
cross-country flight, 27, 29-31

Federal Aviation Administration, 6

ground school, 5

Jenny, 8

Lindbergh, Charles, 34
Los Angeles, 7, 21, 29, 30

manicurist, 12

pilot's license, 5, 9, 15, 21, 22

segregation, 9, 36
sharecropper, 11
stunt, 8, 17, 34

Truman, Harry, 9
Tuskegee Airmen, 9, 36-37
Tuskegee Institute, 33, 41

U.S. Air Force, 37

World War I, 6, 7, 12, 20, 23, 25, 26, 29,
World War II, 36, 37
Wright Brothers, 6

48